WOND'ROUS
FARE

A Calico Book
Published by Contemporary Books, Inc.
180 North Michigan Avenue, Chicago, Illinois 60601
Copyright © 1988 by The Kipling Press
Text copyright © 1988 by Lyn Stallworth
Cover Illustration © 1985 by Peter deSeve
Illustrations Copyright © 1988 by Jim Bennett
Illustrations Copyright © 1988 by Dennis Dittrick
Illustrations Copyright © 1988 by John Hayes
Illustrations Copyright © 1988 by Jim Robinson

Book Design by Jennifer Dubnau
Art Direction by Charlotte Krebs
Library of Congress Catalog Card Number: 88-20368
International Standard Book Number: 0-8092-4481-0
Manufactured in the United States of America

Published simultaneously in Canada by Beaverbooks, Ltd.
195 Allstate Parkway, Valleywood Business Park
Markham, Ontario L3R 4T8 Canada

Library of Congress Cataloging-in-Publication Data

Stallworth, Lyn.
Wond'rous fare.

"Calico book."
Summary: A collection of thirty-six recipes inspired by various
literary sources.
Each recipe is rated on difficulty and accompanied by an
appropriate quote.
1. Cookery—Juvenile literature.   2. Literary cookbooks—
Juvenile literature.
[1. Cookery.   2. Literary cookbooks]   I. Bennett, Jim, 1946-
ill.   II. Title.
TX652.5.S62   1988   641.5′123   88-20368
ISBN 0-8092-4481-0

WOND'ROUS FARE

by Lyn Stallworth

With illustrations by Jim Bennett, Dennis Dittrick, John Hayes, and Jim Robinson

Cover illustration by Peter deSeve

A CALICO BOOK
Published by Contemporary Books, Inc.
CHICAGO · NEW YORK

Contents

Breakfast

Soups & Salads

Main Dishes

Vegetables

Savoury Comforts

Desserts

FOREWORD

I love to cook and I love to read, and I especially like books that have food in them. When I read about Toad's Buttered Toast in THE WIND IN THE WILLOWS, or Beautiful Soup in ALICE IN WONDERLAND, my mouth waters! So it seemed a fine idea to go through some of the best books ever written for children, looking *just* for food, and then turn those descriptions into recipes that young people can cook. Don't expect the recipes always to follow the books exactly—often I used my imagination to make a recipe that I think will please you more.

If this is your first cookbook, let's discuss how you will use it. First, you must read a recipe all the way through so that you know exactly what you have to do, and what you must have ready. Then you get out everything that you will need—the pots and pans, the measuring cups and spoons, and the ingredients you will cook with. If you haven't cooked before, you might start with a simple recipe, like Turtle Egg Feast. Notice that I have labelled each recipe "easy," "medium," or "hard," so that you can start with the simple recipes and move on to the more difficult ones as you get better. You should have an older, experienced cook in the kitchen with you, to help with ovens and stove burners, but you can do all the actual cooking yourself. Oh yes, what is the first thing you do, after you have decided to make a recipe? You put on your apron and you wash your hands. Happy cooking!

Lyn Stallworth

Turtle Egg Feast

Ingredients you will need:

½ cake tofu (bean curd)
2 eggs
1 teaspoon butter
Sprinkle of soy sauce or Chinese
sweet-and-sour sauce

Turtle eggs are very small. In this recipe, the small pieces of tofu take the place of the cooked whites of turtle eggs. You will need a nonstick 8-inch frying pan.

1 Put the cake of tofu on the work surface and cut it in half. Put one half away, covered with water, to use another time. Cut the remaining tofu into ¼-inch pieces.

2 Break the eggs into a small bowl. Stir very well with a fork or chopstick.

3 Put the pan on the stove over medium heat. Put in the butter and turn the heat down to low. When it melts, tip the pan so the butter runs over the surface.

4 Pour in the two eggs and stir them gently with a chopstick or wooden spoon. Now put in the tofu pieces, and keep on stirring, slowly and gently. You want the eggs to be soft but firm, not runny. As soon as they begin to set, turn off the heat and take the pan off the stove. Even though the eggs may not look as though they are cooked enough, you should take them off the heat because the eggs' own heat will keep them cooking for a little while longer.

5 Put an equal amount of Turtle Eggs on 2 plates. Sprinkle with soy sauce, or add some Chinese sauce.

Serves 2

After dinner all the gang turned out to hunt for turtle eggs on the bar. They went about poking sticks into the sand, and when they found a soft place they went down on their knees and dug with their hands. Sometimes they would take fifty or sixty eggs out of one hole. They were perfectly round white things a trifle smaller than an English walnut. They had a famous fried-egg feast that night, and another on Friday morning.

—TOM SAWYER (chapter 7, during Tom's
adventure on the sand bar)

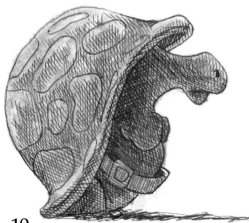

Henny Penny's Pancakes

— THE TALES OF PETER RABBIT

1 Put the butter in an 8-inch frying pan and melt it over low heat. When the butter is melted turn off the heat and move the frying pan to a cold place on the stove.

2 Break the egg over a big bowl and beat it with a fork or a chopstick. Measure the baking powder and add it, then add the sugar. Mix everything together. Add the flour and mix together well. Now pour in the buttermilk and the melted butter and mix again, but not too much—you should have a few lumps in the batter. If you mix too much, you'll get tough pancakes!

3 Don't wash the frying pan, but put it on the stove over medium heat. To know when it is hot enough, flick a drop of water into the pan. When it jumps and sizzles, the pan is ready.

4 Take a ¼-cup measure and fill it with pancake batter. Pour the batter into the pan and tilt the pan so the batter runs all over it. Cook the pancake until the edges get brown and little holes start to appear on top. This takes about 2 minutes. Flip the pancake over and cook until the other side is brown; this takes about 1½ minutes. Keep on making pancakes.

5 Spread the pancakes with your favorite jam and roll them up. Eat them from your hand, like a hot dog.

Makes 4 big pancakes

Ingredients you will need:

1 tablespoon butter or margarine
1 egg
½ teaspoon baking powder
1 teaspoon sugar
½ cup flour
½ cup buttermilk
Your favorite jam

Toad's Buttered Toast

(French Toast)

Ingredients you will need:

1 egg
½ cup milk
2 tablespoons maple or pancake syrup
4 slices bread
4 teaspoons butter
4 teaspoons vegetable oil

1 Use a fork to beat the egg in a dish or pan large enough to lay the bread slices side by side. Beat in the milk and syrup and put the bread in the pan. Turn each piece over. Leave the bread in the egg mixture for at least 5 minutes, until it has "drunk" up all the egg and milk.

2 Cook the French Toast 1 slice at a time. In an 8-inch frying pan (nonstick is best) put 1 teaspoon of butter and 1 teaspoon of oil. The oil keeps the butter from burning. Put the pan over medium heat.

3 When the butter sizzles, use a pancake turner to lift a slice of bread and put it in the pan. Cook for 2 minutes, or until the underside is speckled brown. Turn it very carefully, and cook 2 minutes on the other side. Put the French Toast on a plate, and cook the other slices. If you want very hot French Toast, you can cook 2 slices and eat them, then come back and cook the other 2.

Makes 4 slices

You don't need syrup or butter with the French Toast, because they are in the recipe. But you can add them if you like. This is a good way to use up stale bread.

When the girl returned, some hours later, she carried a tray, with a cup of fragrant tea steaming on it; and a plate piled up with very hot buttered toast, cut thick, very brown on both sides, with the butter running through the holes in it in great golden drops, like honey from the honeycomb.
— THE WIND IN THE WILLOWS
(chapter 8, after Toad has been in jail for reckless driving)

Uncle Ebenezer's Porridge

Ingredients you will need:

¹/₃ cup old-fashioned oatmeal
1 cup water
1 teaspoon sugar
1 tablespoon raisins
Chopped apple bits
Dash cinnamon
Yogurt or milk

1 Cook the oatmeal in the water according to the directions on the box, but add the sugar and raisins at the same time you add the oatmeal to the water. Cover and let stand 3 minutes.

2 While the oatmeal is sitting, covered, chop up some apple, just as much as you want. (About 2 tablespoons is good.) Put the oatmeal in a bowl, cover it with the apple bits, and add a dash of cinnamon.

3 Add some yogurt or milk, and enjoy!

Serves 1
(This recipe may be doubled)

Did you know that Uncle Ebenezer ate his porridge, which is really oatmeal, without milk or sugar, only salt? No wonder he was so mean! The new version is much, much better.

For a day that was begun so ill, the day passed fairly well. We had porridge cold again at noon, and hot porridge at night; porridge and small beer was my uncle's diet.

—David Balfour in KIDNAPPED
(chapter 4, the day
before his uncle tries
to kill him)

13

SOUPS & SALADS

Jack's Beanstalk Salad

Ingredients you will need:

4 slices bacon
½ cup canned or cooked kidney beans
1 cup canned or cooked green beans
1 cup canned or cooked lima beans
¼ cup chopped celery
1 large carrot, peeled and grated
½ cup brown sugar
¼ cup cider vinegar
2 tablespoons vegetable oil

1 Cook the bacon in a frying pan over medium heat, turning it once, until it is crisp. Drain on paper towels. Set aside.

2 If the beans are canned, drain them, put them in a sieve and rinse them under cool water. Put all the beans in a large bowl and add the celery and shredded carrot.

3 Put the sugar and vinegar in a small saucepan. Cook over low heat, stirring with a wooden spoon, just until all the sugar is dissolved. Mix in the oil. Pour the mixture over the beans and vegetables. Crumble the bacon and add it to the bowl. Mix everything together well and chill the salad in the refrigerator for 2 hours or more.

Makes 6 servings

DITTRICH

Beautiful Soup

"Beautiful Soup, so rich and green,
Waiting in a hot tureen!
Who for dainties would not stoop?
Soup of the evening, beautiful Soup!"

—The Mock Turtle in ALICE IN
WONDERLAND ("The Lobster-
Quadrille")

Ingredients you will need:

3 cups chicken broth
3 ounces thin green "angel hair" pasta
or other green noodles (a big
handful of noodles)
¼ cup frozen green peas
1 tablespoon chopped parsley

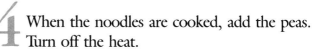

1 If the noodles are long, chop them up so they will be easy to eat.

2 Put the broth in a medium-sized saucepan. Set it on the stove over medium heat. When it begins to boil, add the green noodles. Stir them with a wooden spoon.

3 When you think the noodles are almost cooked, test to make sure. Here is how: fish one of the noodles out with a fork, being careful not to splash yourself. Bite it. If it is hard, put it back and cook the noodles some more.

4 When the noodles are cooked, add the peas. Turn off the heat.

5 Using a pot holder for the handle of the pan and another for the side, take the pan off the stove and put it on a chopping block or other surface that the hot pan won't hurt.

6 With a ladle, divide the soup equally between soup bowls. Sprinkle some parsley on each serving.

Makes 2 or 3 servings

Calabashes of Poe-Poe

A calabash is a gourd that grows on a tree. A dried gourd, cut in half, makes dishes also called calabashes. You can make your own calabashes from a banana.

Ingredients you will need:

1 large ripe banana
8 teaspoons peanut butter
Lettuce leaves
4 teaspoons honey
4 teaspoons coconut flakes
1 small red apple

Their chief food was roasted breadfruit, yams, coconuts, baked pig, mammee-apples, tappa rolls and bananas, washed down with calabashes of poe-poe; but you never exactly knew whether it would be a real meal or just a make-believe, it all depended on Peter's whim.

—PETER PAN (chapter 7, just before the adventure in Mermaid Lagoon)

1 Peel the banana and lay it flat on the cutting board. Cut it in half lengthwise. Cut carefully; take your time. Cut each banana portion in half crosswise.

2 With a teaspoon or melon-baller, hollow out each banana portion to make a long small "boat," or dish. Fill each banana dish with 2 teaspoons of peanut butter.

3 Arrange lettuce leaves on 2 salad plates. On each plate put 2 of the filled banana portions on the lettuce, side by side, with a little space between. Dribble the honey over the peanut butter and sprinkle on the coconut flakes.

4 Cut the apple into wedges. You need only 8 wedges. Put the wedges, red side up, between the bananas.

Serves 2
(This recipe may be doubled)

Fruit Salad by Aladdin

She fetched a napkin and laid in it the magic fruits from the enchanted garden, which sparkled and shone like the most beautiful jewels.

—THE ARABIAN NIGHTS
(from "Aladdin and the Wonderful Lamp")

Ingredients you will need:

cup cold water
packet unflavored gelatin
tablespoons sugar
cup unsweetened grape juice
tablespoon fresh lemon juice
Miniature marshmallows

1 Measure ¼ cup of cold water from the tap and put it into a medium-sized mixing bowl. Sprinkle the gelatin over it.

2 Put ¾ cup water into a small saucepan and bring it to a boil over medium heat. When the water is boiling, pour it over the gelatin. (An adult should help with this.) Add the sugar, grape juice, and lemon juice. Stir.

3 Rinse two miniature muffin tins with cold water, turn them upside down, and shake them over the sink. Put them on a cookie sheet, right side up.

4 Use the ¼-cup measure to fill the muffin tins with the gelatin and juice mixture. Fill the cups almost full. Put the cookie sheet in the refrigerator.

5 When you are ready to eat the little "jewels," you have to unmold them. Fill the sink with 2 inches of hot water. Take one of the muffin pans by the ends, and dip the bottom of the pan into the hot water. Count to 5, slowly. Shake the pan; the gelatin molds should start to wobble.

6 Now you have to turn them out of the molds. Turn the cookie sheet over and put it on top of a muffin pan. Put one hand under the pan, and one on top of the cookie sheet. Grip hard, because you are going to flip the pan over. Now flip it gently. Shake the upside-down pan back and forth, to loosen the gelatin, without lifting the pan. Now lift it up gently from both sides; the molds should slide out. If they don't, you must wring out a dish towel in hot water and put it over the upturned pan for a few seconds. When the molds are free, use a pancake turner to slide them onto plates. You now have beautiful jewels with a surprise inside!

Makes 24

MAIN DISHES

Ben Gunn Toasted Cheese

Ingredients you will need:

2 slices bread
2 tablespoons chili sauce or ketchup
2 tablespoons sweet pickle relish
4 slices cheddar cheese

"Marooned three years agone," he continued, "and lived on goats since then, and berries, and oysters. Wherever a man is, says I, a man can do for himself. But, mate, my heart is sore for Christian diet. You mightn't happen to have a piece of cheese about you, now? No? Well, many's the long night I've dreamed of cheese—toasted, mostly,—and woke up again and here I were."

—Crazy Ben Gunn in TREASURE ISLAND
(chapter 15, during Jim Hawkins'
escape from Long John)

1 Tear off a sheet of aluminum foil large enough to put the slices of bread on. If you are using an oven broiler, put the foil on a cookie sheet and preheat the broiler. If you are using a toaster oven, lay the foil on the broiler tray. Smear butter or oil on the foil so the bread won't stick. (You can also make Toasted Cheese in the microwave. In that case, put a sheet of waxed paper in the microwave oven.)

2 Toast the slices of bread. On each slice, spread 1 tablespoon of ketchup. On top of that spread 1 tablespoon of sweet pickle relish. Lay 2 slices of cheese on each slice of bread.

3 Put the cheese on the prepared foil or in the microwave, and cook just until the cheese bubbles.

Makes 2 servings

King of Tarts Ham Sandwich

Ingredients you will need:

2 tablespoons mayonnaise
2 tablespoons ketchup
1 ripe tomato
4 pita pockets
4 slices boiled ham or sliced turkey
   breast
1 cup loosely packed alfalfa sprouts

In this recipe we have both ham and hay. Hay? Yes indeed. Alfalfa is a kind of hay!

"You alarm me!" said the King. "I feel faint—Give me a ham sandwich!" On which the Messenger, to Alice's great amusement, opened a bag that hung round his neck, and handed a sandwich to the King, who devoured it greedily.

"Another sandwich!" said the King.

"There's nothing left but hay now," the Messenger said, peeping into the bag.

"Hay, then," the King murmured in a faint whisper.

THROUGH THE LOOKING GLASS (chapter 7)

1 Put the mayonnaise and ketchup in a small bowl and mix them together.

2 Slice the tomato into 4 thick slices.

3 Open the pita pockets. With a spoon or table knife put an equal amount of the mayonnaise-ketchup mixture into each one.

4 Fill the pita pockets. In each one put a slice of ham or turkey and a slice of tomato.

5 Stuff an equal amount of alfalfa sprouts into each pocket.

Serves 4

Flamingo Stew

—SWISS FAMILY ROBINSON

Ingredients you will need:

1 2-ounce package corn chips (about 1½ cups)
1 6½-ounce can tuna fish
1 can condensed cheddar cheese soup
3 tablespoons tomato sauce

Preheat the oven to 350 degrees.

1 Get a small baking dish, about 6 inches wide and 2 inches high, and coat it with butter, oil, or vegetable spray. Set it aside.

2 Put the corn chips in a big paper bag. Twist the bag shut. Crush the corn chips lightly with a rolling pin. You will have both crumbs and larger pieces; that is all right.

3 Drain the can of tuna fish. Put it in a big mixing bowl and pull it apart with a fork. This is called "flaking."

4 Mix the cheddar cheese soup and the tomato sauce into the tuna fish. Mix in the corn chip pieces.

5 Put the mixture into the prepared baking dish. Bake in the center of the oven for 30 minutes, uncovered.

Serves 3 or 4

It was, indeed, the most beautiful stew in the world, being made of partridges, and pheasants, and chickens, and hares, and rabbits, and peahens, and guineafowls, and one or two other things. Toad took the plate on his lap, almost crying, and stuffed, and stuffed, and stuffed, and kept asking for more, and the gypsy never grudged it him.

—THE WIND IN THE WILLOWS
(chapter 10, when Toad is traveling in disguise)

Gypsy Stew

Ingredients you will need:

1 cup flour
¼ teaspoon salt
1 cup milk
2 eggs
½ pound (8 ounces) brown-and-serve breakfast sausages
2 tablespoons vegetable oil

Preheat the oven to 400 degrees.

A wonderful dish for lunch or supper, too. Another name for it is Toad in the Hole. That is because the sausages look as though they are hiding!

1 In a big mixing bowl, put the flour, salt, and milk. Mix them around with a fork. Now break the eggs into the bowl.

2 Use a rotary eggbeater or a hand-held electric beater to mix everything together until very smooth. (Practice first with a bowl of water if this is your first time with beaters.) If you need to, scrape around the edge of the bowl with a rubber scraper so all the ingredients can be mixed evenly. Set aside for a minute.

3 Brown the sausages according to the directions on the package. Put the oil in a shallow 8-inch square or round pan. Put the sausages in the pan, a little bit apart, and pour the batter over them.

4 Bake the dish in the center of the oven for 30 minutes, until the batter is browned and puffed way up over the edge of the pan.

Serves 4

VEGETABLES

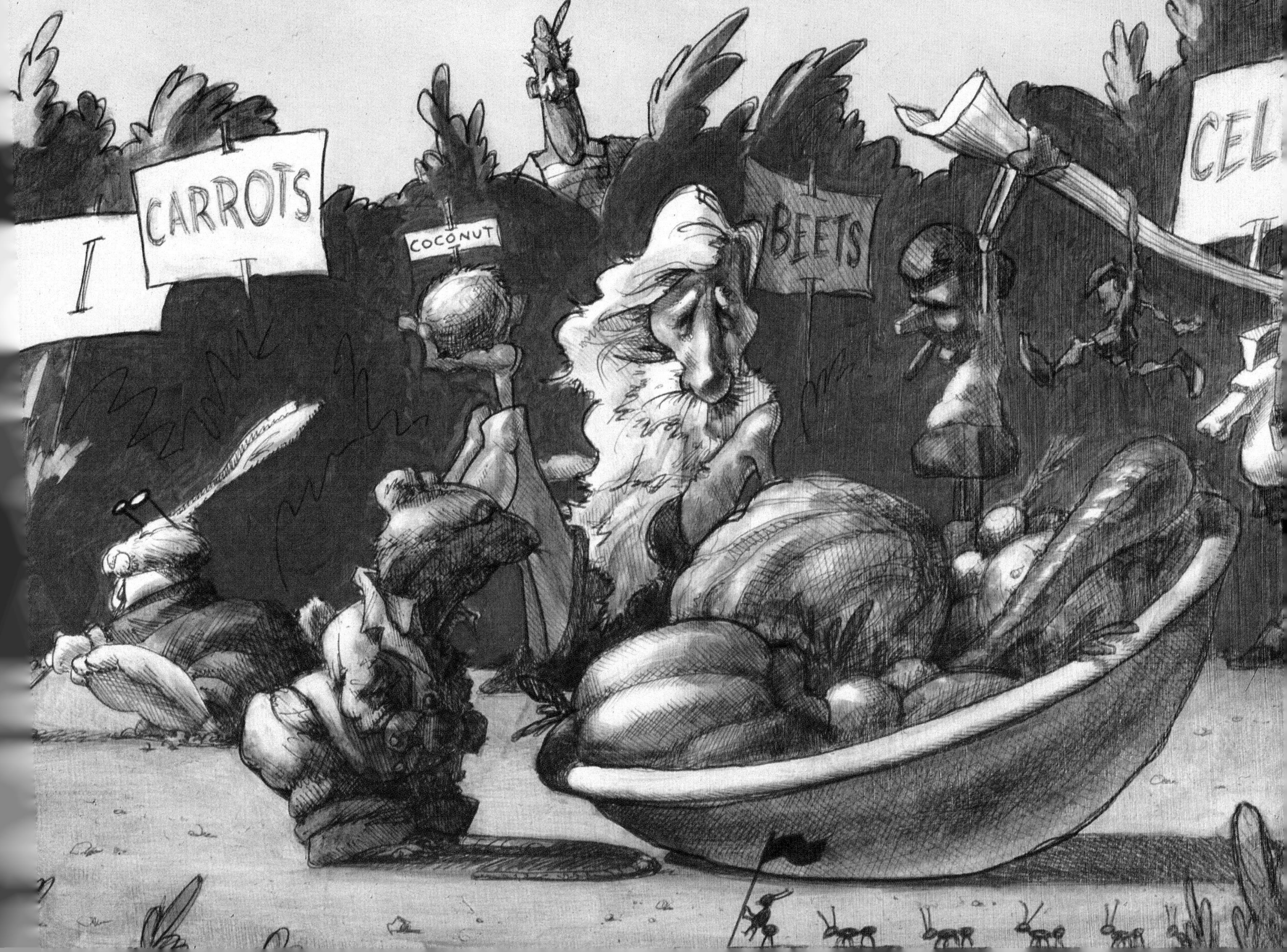

Mole's Garden Mixture
(with Onion Sauce)

—THE WIND IN THE WILLOWS

Ingredients for Garden Mixture:

Fresh raw vegetables, such as carrot and celery sticks, cucumber slices, cherry tomatoes, broccoli florets, and cauliflower florets.

Ingredients for Onion Sauce:

1 small scallion (spring onion)
1 3-ounce package cream cheese
¼ cup sour cream
¼ cup cream or milk
1 tablespoon parsley flakes, if you want them

1 Arrange the vegetables nicely on a platter, and serve with a bowl of delicious Onion Sauce (see steps 2–5) to dip the vegetables in.

This is a delicious dip for raw vegetables, mild and not too oniony. Grown-ups like it too, so make it when they have a party! You will need a blender.

2 Wash the scallion and cut off the root end and most of the green part. Peel off 1 layer and cut the scallion in 6 pieces. Put it in the blender.

3 Cut the cream cheese in 6 pieces and put them in the blender. Pour in the sour cream and cream.

4 If you want the sauce to be pale green, add the parsley leaves. They are only for color—you can't really taste them.

5 Put the blender lid on tightly and blend until the Onion Sauce is very, very smooth.

Makes ¾ cup

Clara's Green Bean Casserole

—HEIDI

Ingredients you will need:

3 slices white bread
Butter
1 cup cooked green beans
1 cup grated Swiss cheese
2 eggs
1 cup milk

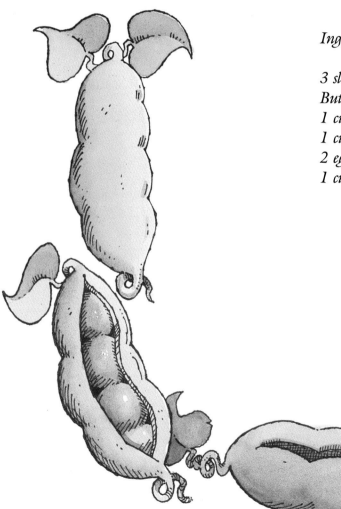

Preheat the oven to 350 degrees.

1 Get out a small, shallow casserole dish. Butter the slices of bread and cut them into cubes. Put the cubes in the casserole, and spread them out.

2 If you have cooked fresh or frozen green beans, drain them well. (Leftover beans should be drained if they are in liquid.) Arrange them over the bread cubes.

3 Sprinkle the grated cheese on evenly.

4 Break the eggs into a mixing bowl. Beat them well with a fork or a rotary beater. Add the milk and beat again.

5 Pour the egg-milk mixture evenly over the casserole. Bake in the center of the oven for 30–35 minutes, until puffy and lightly browned.

Serves 4

Mrs. Cratchit's Slow Potatoes

Ingredients you will need:

5 medium yams or sweet potatoes
5 tablespoons butter
3 tablespoons dark corn syrup
¼ teaspoon salt
2 tablespoons honey
¼ cup brown sugar
Marshmallows

1 Peel the yams and boil them in water until they are barely tender—that is, when a fork will pierce them but they are still a little hard. Drain them and let them cool.

Preheat the oven to 350 degrees.

2 When the yams are cool enough to handle, cut them in ¼-inch slices. Use 2 tablespoons of the butter to smear the bottom and sides of an 8-inch square baking dish. Arrange the sliced yams in the dish.

3 In a saucepan put the corn syrup, salt, honey, the rest of the butter, and the brown sugar. Heat the mixture, stirring with a wooden spoon, until the sugar melts. Pour the sauce over the yam slices.

4 Cover the baking dish with aluminum foil and bake for 30 minutes.

5 Remove the dish from the oven and carefully take the foil off, opening it from the back so you don't get steam in your face.

6 With a fork, mash the yams together well. Cover them with marshmallows. Put the dish back in the oven and cook 20 to 25 minutes more, or until the marshmallows are toasted.

Makes 6 servings

...these young Cratchits danced about the table, and exalted Master Peter Cratchit to the skies, while he (not proud, though his collars nearly choked him) blew the fire, until the slow potatoes bubbling up, knocked loudly at the saucepan-lid to be let out and peeled.

—A CHRISTMAS CAROL
(stave 3, just before the Cratchits' sad Christmas dinner)

Diet Lizard

The Fox would have been glad to order something, but his doctor had ordered a strict diet for him. He had to content himself with a tender young rabbit dressed with chicken giblets. After the rabbit he topped off with a few partridges, pheasants, frogs, lizards, and some grapes. That was all he could eat. The very sight of food, he said, was distasteful to him, and he didn't want another mouthful.

—PINOCCHIO (chapter 13, at the Red Lobster Inn)

Ingredients you will need:

small, very ripe avocado
lemon, cut in half
small capers (tiny round pickles)
Orange slices or sections
French dressing

1 With a sharp knife, cut the avocado in half lengthwise. Take out the big seed and, with a teaspoon, scrape away any brown stuff you see. Immediately squeeze lemon juice on the cut avocado halves to keep them from turning dark.

2 With a regular tablespoon, very carefully run around the peel of one of the avocado halves and lift out the flesh. Try to keep it in one piece. Squeeze on lemon juice.

3 Have two plates ready. Cut the avocado half down the middle, using a regular table knife. Then cut off a little of the underside so the two pieces will lie flat on the plates. These will be the bodies of the lizards. Put one body on each plate.

4 Lift the flesh out of the other avocado half and squeeze on lemon juice. Cut long, thin slices to form the tails. Put them in place. Remember, sprinkle with lemon juice!

5 Cut more pieces to be the arms and legs, and put them in place. At the top, thinner end of the lizard bodies, put two capers on each. These will be the eyes.

6 Put the orange slices or sections around the lizards. Cover with as much French dressing or other dressing as you like.

Serves 2

SAVOURY COMFORTS

Ratty's Picnic Ecstasy

"There's cold chicken inside it, . . . cold tongue cold ham cold beef pickled gherkins salad french rollscressandwichespottedmeatgingerbeer lemonadesodawater—"

"Oh stop, stop," cried Mole in ecstasies. "This is too much!"

—WIND IN THE WILLOWS
(chapter 1, Ratty reciting the contents of his picnic basket)

Have a cold, delicious, nourishing drink! To make the drink, you have to start the night before.

Ingredients you will need:

1 ripe banana
1 cup milk
2 tablespoons maple syrup or other syrup
1 teaspoon fresh lemon juice

1 Peel the banana, cut it into 6 chunks and wrap well in plastic wrap. Put in the freezer overnight.

2 The following day, set up the blender. Put all ingredients on the counter.

3 Put the frozen banana chunks, milk, syrup, and lemon juice in the blender. Whirl until the drink is smooth.

Serves 1

Long John Silver's Rum

A "pinch" is a small amount, just as much as you can pick up between your thumb and forefinger.

Ingredients you will need:

2 sugar lumps
2 cups cider or apple juice
Pinch cinnamon
Pinch cloves
Pinch nutmeg
2 lemon slices
2 orange slices
2 long cinnamon sticks

1 Put the sugar lumps on the bottom of 2 cups.

2 Put the rest of the ingredients in a small saucepan. Cook over medium heat, stirring with a wooden spoon and mashing down on the lemon and orange slices, until the cider bubbles. Let it boil gently for 2 minutes.

3 Fish out the fruit slices and cinnamon sticks, and pour the Spiced Rum into the 2 cups. Use the cinnamon sticks to mash up the sugar lumps.

Makes 2 cups

I'm a plain man; rum and bacon and eggs is what I want, and that head up there for to watch ships off.

-Bill Bowes in TREASURE ISLAND
(chapter 1, just as he arrives at
Jim Hawkins' home)

35

Summer Orchard

—THE WIND IN THE WILLOWS

Ingredients you will need:

2 firm ripe pears
2 small apples
½ cup water
2 tablespoons brown sugar

1 When you use a food mill, you don't have to peel the fruit. The peels stay behind as you force the sauce through the holes. Cut the pears in half lengthwise, then in quarters. Trim away the seeds and cut off the stems. Cut the apples in quarters and trim them.

2 Put the pears, apples, water, and brown sugar in a small saucepan. Put the saucepan on the stove and turn the heat to medium. Cover the pan. When you hear noises, that means the water is beginning to boil, so set the kitchen timer for 15 minutes. Turn the heat to low so that the mixture bubbles gently.

Sauce

To make this recipe you should have a Foley or other kind of food mill. A food mill has a blade that turns and presses soft food through holes, like a sieve. A food mill is great for mashed potatoes, too.

3 After 5 minutes, lift the lid and stir the fruit with a wooden spoon. Start to mash it as much as you can—most of it will still be hard. After another 5 minutes, lift the lid again and mash. Does the fruit look dry? If so, add a little water—not too much. Wait another 5 minutes, and mash again.

4 After 15 minutes, the fruit should be soft. However, some pears and apples are harder than others, so you may have to cook your sauce longer. If so, add a little more water and cook until soft.

5 Turn off the heat and let the sauce cool. Hot fruit can burn you.

6 When the fruit is cool, use a rubber spatula to scrape it into the food mill that you have placed over a bowl. Force all the fruit mixture through the holes, stopping once in a while to scrape the fruit down under the blade with the rubber spatula. You can eat the Summer Orchard Sauce as it is, or with ice cream.

Makes 1½ cups or more

Pecos Bill's Chili

—PECOS BILL

1 Cut off the ends of the onion. Peel it and cut it in half. Put the 2 halves on a work surface, flat side down. Chop the onion as fine as you can.

2 Peel the garlic clove and chop it.

3 Put the oil in the pan. Add the chopped onion and garlic. Turn the heat to medium. Cook, stirring with a wooden spoon, for 5 minutes, or until the onion bits are wilted and you can almost see through them. Now add the meat.

4 Stir the meat, turning it over and mashing it with the wooden spoon for about 8 minutes, until none of the pink color is left.

5 Stir in the tomato puree, salt, sugar, chili powder, and oregano. Mix well. When the sauce begins to bubble, turn the heat to low. It should bubble gently, never boil hard. Stir often, and check to see that it doesn't cook too fast. Don't cover it. You needn't stand over it the whole time, but keep an eye on it. If it looks dry, stir in 2 tablespoons of water. Cook for 45 minutes.

6 Stir in the oregano and the drained beans. Cook 15 minutes more. Serve with taco shells or boiled rice.

Ingredients you will need:

1 medium onion
1 clove garlic
1 tablespoon vegetable oil
1 pound chopped chuck (hamburger meat)
2 cups canned tomato puree
½ teaspoon salt
2 teaspoons sugar
1 tablespoon mild chili powder
½ teaspoon oregano
1 can pinto beans, drained

Make this chili in a 12-inch wide nonstick frying pan.

Makes 6 servings

DESSERTS

Field Mouse Favorite

—THE TALES OF PETER RABBIT

Ingredients you will need:

3 cups old-fashioned oatmeal
1½ cups sweetened shredded coconut
½ cup wheat germ
½ cup sesame seeds
½ cup sunflower seeds
¼ cup vegetable oil
½ cup honey
½ cup cold water
1 cup honey-roasted peanuts
½ cup raisins

Preheat the oven to 225 degrees.

1 In a large bowl mix together the oatmeal, coconut, wheat germ, sesame seeds, and sunflower seeds. Add the oil, honey, and water, and stir well with a wooden spoon.

2 Oil a large jelly roll pan. Spread the mixture out in it and put it in the oven. Bake for 1½ hours, stirring often. Stir in the peanuts and bake 1 hour more, stirring often, until the granola is crisp and dry. When cool, mix in the raisins.

Makes about 5 cups

Friday's Fruit Bowl

Ingredients you will need:

2 small tangerines or 1 temple orange
1 tablespoon semisweet chocolate chips

Here is how Friday made the Fruit Bowl when cocoa and orange trees were in bloom. With it you should drink a tall glass of ice-cold limeade.

1 Peel the tangerines or orange. Pull off all the white strings. Separate the sections and put them, close together, on a small plate.

2 Cover the sections with the chocolate chips. Put the dish in the microwave or toaster oven just long enough for the chocolate chips to get soft; they should not melt or change shape. Eat with a knife and fork or your fingers.

Serves 1

> *I saw here abundance of cocoa trees, orange and lemon and citron trees . . . However, the green limes that I gathered were not only pleasant to eat, but very wholesome; and I mixed their juice afterwards with water, which made it very wholesome and very cool and refreshing.*
>
> —ROBINSON CRUSOE
> ("The Journal: Recovery")

43

Becky's Wedding Cake

These little cakes are really fun to make, and if a grown-up melts the chocolate, even little kids can do it.

Ingredients you will need:

1½ cups granola cereal
⅓ cup dark corn syrup
1 cup chunky peanut butter
1 cup semisweet chocolate chips

1 Line a jelly-roll pan with a sheet of waxed paper.

2 Put the granola, corn syrup, and peanut butter in a mixing bowl . Mix it all very well with a wooden spoon.

3 Put the chocolate bits in a small saucepan. Put 2 inches of water in a larger saucepan and put the pan on the stove over medium heat. Put the smaller saucepan with the chocolate in the bigger pan. The hot water will melt the chocolate without letting it burn. Watch it carefully; when the chocolate looks soft, stir it with a wooden spoon. Lift the small pan out of the water and put it on a burn-proof surface to cool.

4 With your hands, make 2-inch-wide balls from the granola mixture, and put them, not touching, on the lined jelly roll pan. You can make 8 balls this size, or smaller ones if you like. You can also pat the mixture into a rectangle, about 4 inches × 10 inches × ½ inch high, if you want to make granola bars.

5 The chocolate should be cool, but still runny enough to spread. With a rubber spatula or with your hands, spread it all over the balls or the rectangle. Put the jelly roll pan in the refrigerator for 30 minutes or longer.

Serves 12 or more

"Tom, I am so hungry!"
Tom took something out of his pocket.
"Do you remember this?" said he.
Becky almost smiled.

"It's our wedding cake, Tom."
"Yes—I wish it was as big as a barrel, for it's all we've got."
—TOM SAWYER (chapter 31, when Becky and Tom are hopelessly lost in the caves)

Agib's Sweetmeats

We then sat down to a supper of dried fruits and sweetmeats, after which some sang and others danced.

—THE ARABIAN NIGHTS
(from "The Story of the
Third Calendar")

Ingredients you will need:

2 cups mixed soft, dried fruits
1 cup orange juice
1 strip of lemon peel
4 tablespoons honey

1 Put the dried fruit in a small saucepan and cover with the orange juice. Add the lemon peel and honey, and stir with a wooden spoon. Set over medium heat. When the orange juice begins to boil, lower the heat so that it just bubbles. Cook, uncovered, for about 25 minutes. Watch to see that there is enough juice; if the juice is cooking away, add more by the tablespoon. Stir the fruit often.

2 After 25 minutes, the fruit should be plump and juicy, and the orange juice absorbed. If there is still a lot of juice, raise the heat and cook it away, about 5 minutes. Stir the fruit gently with a wooden spoon. Use a potholder to grasp the handle of the pan and move it off the heat to another place on the stove. Be very careful, because hot fruit is really hot and can burn you. Let the fruit cool.

3 Spread the fruit out on waxed paper and let it dry a little. The longer it dries, the nicer it gets. (You can also cover it with plastic wrap and put it in the refrigerator.) Eat it with a spoon or with your fingers. Candied sweetmeats are good!

Makes 2 cups

Oaten Cakes

Ingredients you will need:

1 egg
1 cup flour
¼ teaspoon baking soda
¼ teaspoon salt
1 stick (8 tablespoons) butter at room
    temperature
¾ cup firmly packed light brown sugar
½ teaspoon vanilla
2 cups old-fashioned oatmeal

Preheat the oven to 375 degrees.

1 Crack the egg carefully into a small cup. Set it aside.

2 Get a big mixing bowl. Put the flour, baking soda, and salt into a sifter and sift them into the bowl.

3 Put the softened butter and sugar into a medium mixing bowl. Wet a dish towel, wring it out, and fold it. Put the folded towel under the bowl—it will keep it from sliding around as you mix. Using an electric mixer, beat the butter and sugar together until light and fluffy. (If you have never used an electric mixer before, practice first with plain water. Then, if you splatter, no harm is done! You will soon get the hang of it.)

4 Add the egg and vanilla and beat them in well. Add the flour, baking soda, and salt. When the mixture is smooth, stop beating. Put in the oatmeal and mix it in with a wooden spoon to make a firm dough.

5 Have ready 2 ungreased cookie sheets. Put a heaping tablespoon of dough on a cookie sheet. Put 12 of these on each cookie sheet, 2 inches apart. You now have 24 little mounds.

6 Smash each one down lightly with the palm of your hand. Put one cookie sheet in the center of the oven and bake for 8 minutes. Ask for help to remove the cookie sheet from the oven. The Oaten Cakes should look bubbly when you take them out—never mind, they will firm up as they cool. Let them harden on the cookie sheet for 2 minutes, then transfer them to cake racks with a pancake turner.

7 Bake the second batch of Oaten Cakes.

8 Put the rest of the dough on a cooled cookie sheet just as you did in step 5, and bake.

Makes about 34 cookies

"Why," quoth the Beggar, peeping into the mouths of his bags, "I find here a goodly piece of pigeon pie, wrapped in a cabbage leaf to hold the gravy. Here I behold a dainty streaked piece of brawn, and here a fair lump of white bread. Here I find four oaten cakes and a cold knuckle of ham. Ha! In sooth, 'tis strange; but here I behold six eggs that must have come by accident from some poultry hereabouts. They are raw, but roasted upon the coals and spread with a piece of butter that I see—"

—THE ADVENTURES OF ROBIN HOOD
  (from "Robin Turns Beggar")